THIS COLORING BOOK
BELONGS TO:

____

____

THANKS FOR CHOOSING
"Mindful Moments"

"A Self-Care Coloring Book for Anxiety Relief and Mental Health Awareness"

For your convenience, each design is printed single side so colors don't bleed. Still, some pen and makers may stain through. Just place a sheet of paper underneath the page you will be coloring for more better and neat experience.

COLOR TEST PAGE

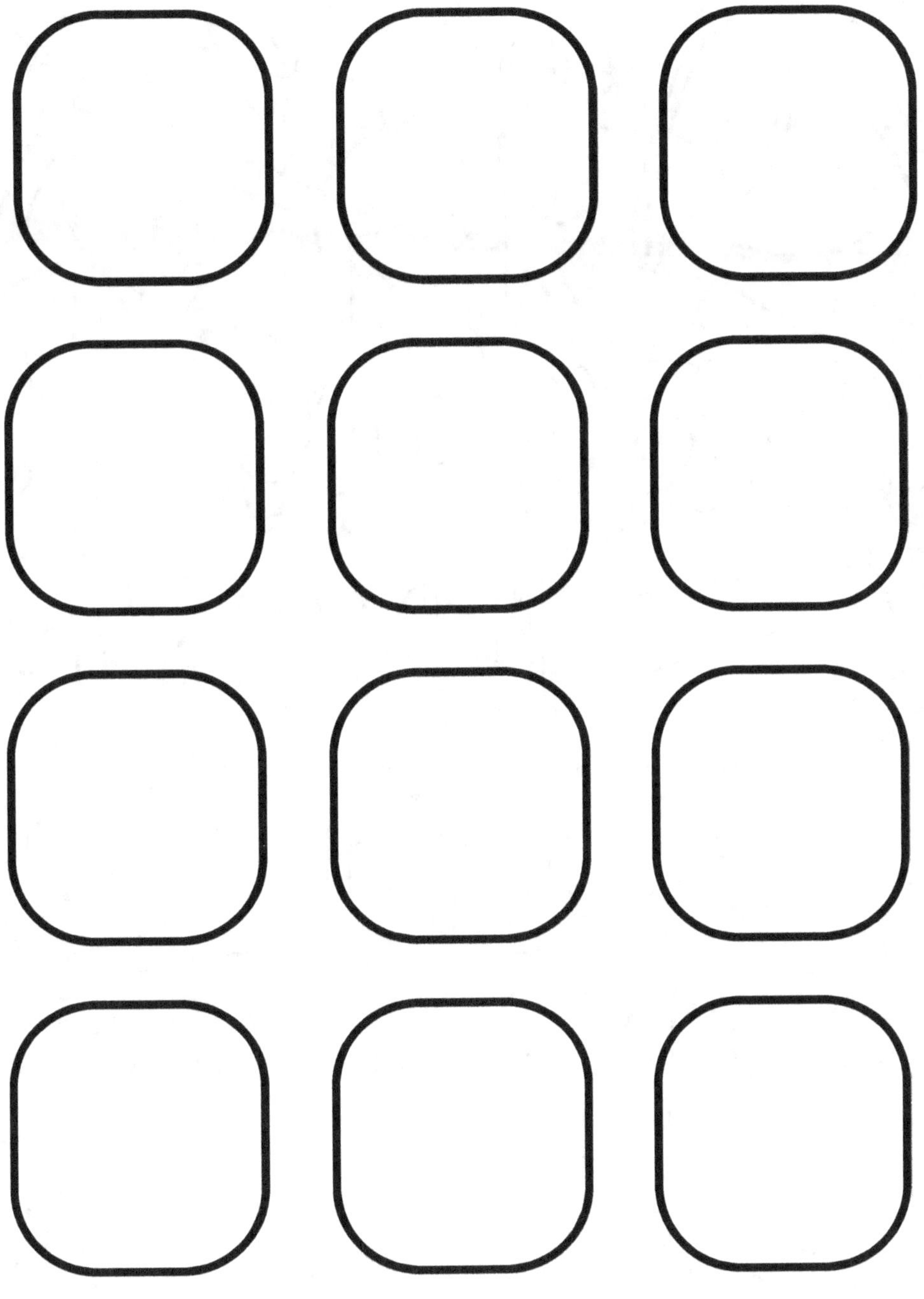

You are
worthy of
love
and
happiness

Take a
DEEP
BREATH
&
find your
calm

Embrace
the
present
moment.

IT'S OKAY
TO TAKE
THINGS
ONE STEP
AT A
TIME.

Your
feelings
ARE
valid
and
important

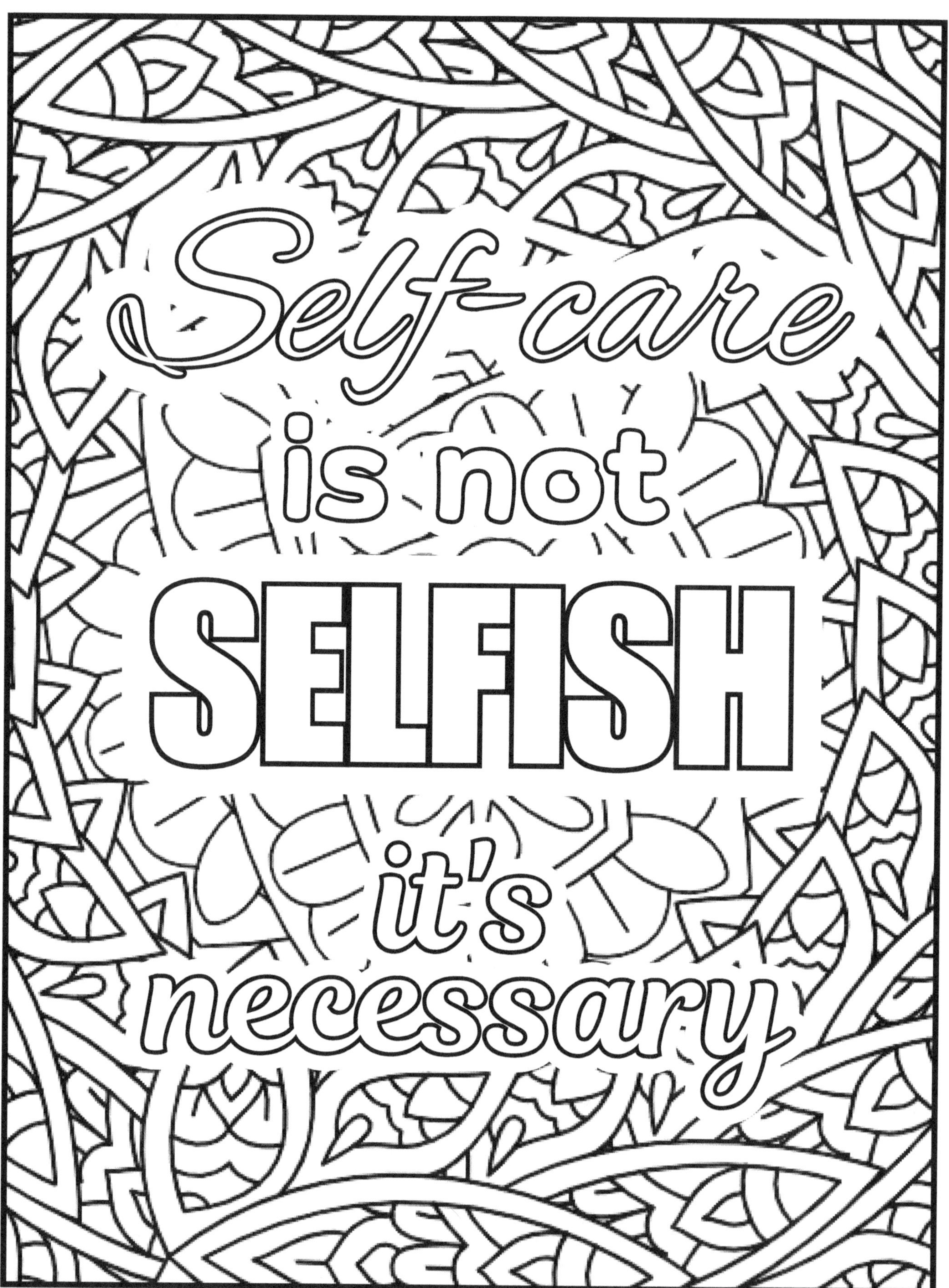

Self-care
is not
SELFISH
it's
necessary

You have the STRENGTH to overcome challenges

PEACE
begins
with a
DEEP
BREATH

Be
gentle
with
yourself
today

HEALING
is a
JOURNEY,
not a
DESTINATION

Find
Joy
in the
little
things

YOU ARE
ENOUGH
JUST AS
YOU ARE

Let go
of what
you
cannot
CONTROL

FIND
BEAUTY
IN
SIMPLICITY

YOU
DESERVE
TO FEEL
AT
PEACE

Nurture your MIND, BODY, AND SOUL

Choose
kindness,
especially
towards
yourself.

It's
okay to
ask for
help

Take
time to
rest and
recharge

You are capable of amazing things

Believe in your ability to heal

Find
solace in
nature
and its
beauty.

Trust
the
process
of
growth

YOU
ARE NOT
ALONE
IN YOUR
STRUGGLES

Embrace
your
IMPERFE
-CTIONS

Your
mental
health
matters

Cultivate
gratitude
and
watch
your
worries
fade

You are
resilient
and
strong

Find
peace
in
your
breath

Prioritize
your
well-
being

Every day is a new beginning

Allow yourself to feel all emotions

You are
deserving
of inner
peace

Take
time to
reflect
and
grow

Practice
self-
compassion
daily

YOUR
JOURNEY IS
UNIQUE
AND
IMPORTANT

Find comfort in your own company

It's
okay to
take a
break

Find
strength
in
vulnerability

Your
peace
is
your
power

Celebrate
your
small
victories.

You have the power to create change

Find joy in
the
journey,
not just
the
destination

Your well-being is a priority

LET
YOUR
MIND BE
STILL
AND AT
EASE

Practice gratitude to cultivate peace

You are
stronger
than you
think

Embrace
the quiet
moments

You are
deserving
of
self-care

Remember, you are worthy of

LOVE, PEACE, AND HAPPINESS.

Take time to nurture your

MIND AND SOUL